THE POWER OF PROFESSIONAL CLOSENESS

THE
POWER
—— OF ——
PROFESSIONAL
CLOSENESS

A GUIDE TO TAKING A HOLISTIC
APPROACH TO YOUR BUSINESS

GOVERT van SANDWIJK

LIONCREST
PUBLISHING

THE POWER OF PROFESSIONAL CLOSENESS

A Guide to Taking a Holistic Approach to Your Business

ISBN   978-1-5445-0226-7 *Paperback*

978-1-5445-0227-4 *Ebook*

For my love, Nicolien,
and dearest daughter and son,
Isa and Tycho

CONTENTS

INTRODUCTION

I first discovered the concept of Professional Closeness—a human mindset applied to business that we'll unpack deeply and actionably in the pages of this book—by becoming painfully aware of its inverse. By staring it in the face, both on the job and at home. It was a complete accident, and it would be years before I could put a name to the phenomenon.

I was twenty-six years old, and I'd started my first serious job: I was employed as a junior psychologist for a small psychological firm. It had been tasked by the court system with determining whether or not suspected criminals had any type of psychopathology that needed to be taken into account in sentencing. Although my primary training was in organizational psychology, the market for psychologists was tough, and I saw this job as a huge opportunity.

I was eager to learn and interested in the field, but there was something I couldn't shake.

In cases involving a particular set of allegations, I found myself assessing suspect after suspect—interviewing them, testing them—all the while thinking, "This person has probably done something very wrong." This feeling wasn't purely an occupational hazard; it also had to do with the fact that I'd just become a father to my firstborn, a baby girl.

I struggled. I felt I couldn't cope or function in a professional manner. Because as a psychologist I was trained, almost indoctrinated, to at all times maintain my objectivity. Yet I couldn't shake those thoughts and emotions about the person I was expected to objectively assess. Looking back, it was a realization that as a person, I function poorly when I am put in a position that forces me to be fully objective—keeping my emotions at bay.

Over time, I became more self-aware and recognized that in situations that force complete objectivity, I was not able to use all my capacities as a professional and a human being. I did find a far better fit for my skillset—which we'll discuss shortly—but that early experience in my career gave way to larger questions: If insights and intuitions are sources of information, should we ignore them in the workplace? Is that even possible to behave in this way and produce the best results?

The answers, I've come to learn, are no and no. **People— whether your employees, executive leaders, or clients—are still just that: people.** And people have more than just a rational perspective. There is an emotional part of the brain that governs our thoughts and actions, too. When both the cognitive *and* intuitive brain are engaged, collaboration becomes more personal and more productive. **Nothing ever gets done in real life with only one side of the story.**

When we approach our work with a mindset of Professional Closeness, more than just personal walls come down: silos in your organization come down, allowing you to take a holistic approach to your business. Communication barriers come down, allowing you to persuade, lead, and interact with those around you in a more meaningful and impactful way. What goes up, you ask? The appeal of your working climate, your sense of purpose and community, and the strength of conversations and the collaboration you have with your team and clients. All of this trickles down into other areas, such as organizational performance, productivity, and business results.

A NEW WORLD

Today, I work with many clients in senior leadership roles who are facing challenges in their organizations, and that may be true for you, too. Perhaps you're struggling to lead in today's ambiguous changing business landscape, where everything is far more technology-driven and connected than it was when you went to business school. **The crux of the old-school management style was an increased level of predictability; those who were the best at predicting, then, were the most successful. That doesn't fly anymore.**

On one side, the context we all work and live in is becoming increasingly unpredictable. On the other hand, especially as automation continues its climb into our everyday lives, some parts of our lives become very predictable. Given this dynamic, how do you use that knowledge to propel your company into the future? And what about the elements that are still unpredictable? How do you handle those?

Maybe you're trying to innovate in ways that move the needle, but you're finding it challenging to gain buy-in and generate ideas that are, in fact, novel. Maybe you are tired of trying to solve problems in an organization where it feels like key stakeholders are moving in different directions. Or, as a symptom of a larger issue, where they are each trying to solve different problems in the first place. Perhaps you have built a strong leadership team, but communication has broken down and there is a lack of cohesion among key segments of your business.

In all of the above scenarios, remember one key factor:

you're still human. These challenges feel heavy. The solutions are unclear to you at the moment, so the emotional side of your brain—which we will discuss in depth in Chapter Two—is wondering, "Is this safe?" Your protective behaviors are likely stagnating your efforts because, at the end of the day, you are still tasked with leading your organization and serving your clients. It's a pressure cooker.

Ultimately, when it comes to leading your organization, perhaps you've started to recognize that the seas have changed while you've been sailing the ship. If this is you, you may have found yourself in increasingly rougher waters trying to steer the company in the right direction.

I have good news: it can be done. In fact, it is being done by organizations all over the globe. Organizations whose leaders have found ways to thrive in an environment that is predictably unpredictable. These leaders have discovered how to bring different functionalities of their businesses together for the greater good, often using technology to eliminate smaller tasks and enable the heart of their company—the people—to bring new ideas to the table. They've been able to become more effective leaders, too, by focusing on context and operating from a mindset of Professional Closeness. At the end of the day, they've not only been able to steer their ships through choppy water, but they've been able to keep them on course and move ahead after the initial storms have passed.

How? Keep reading.

HOW TO USE THIS BOOK

In this book, I will share what I've learned from twenty-plus years of coaching management, executive teams, and assessing and training leaders here in the Netherlands—and, over the last ten years, all over the globe. While it wasn't clear to me at twenty-six, it is abundantly clear to me today: leveraging the power of Professional Closeness benefits you, your team, and your company. Approaching your business in a holistic way is not touchy-feely, and it is not a weakness; it is a strategy rooted in strength, and one I've used to help bring results to my clients from the Congo to Sydney. **After all, although we all have our differences, we share many of the same basic needs regardless of location or culture. At its core, Professional Closeness respects and leverages these commonalities.**

In the following pages, I'll take you on a journey and show you both the scientific and anecdotal proof behind the power of Professional Closeness. I'll also provide insights and tools to help you develop yourself as a leader who can work from this powerful mindset. Last but definitely not least, I'll provide strategies you can use to implement these changes into your business so that it brings your teams together, not further silos them. Don't be fooled: this book is not a collection of concepts and theories. Rather, it is a tool you can use to improve your life and your organization.

Thank you for being here. Let's begin.

PART I

PROFESSIONAL CLOSENESS: WHAT IT IS AND WHY IT MATTERS

CHAPTER ONE

WHAT IS PROFESSIONAL CLOSENESS?

I vividly recall learning about a set of experiments from the 1950s—the Milgram Experiments—for which researchers recruited students for two tasks: being interrogated themselves and being the interrogators. The goal of the study was to determine how far people would go in applying physical pain. The Cliffs Notes? Ultimately, scientists discovered study participants found it shockingly easy to inflict pain upon others if there was physical distance between them. The experiment would be considered unethical by today's standards, yes, but it still sheds a light relevant to the climate in many organizations today. This is it: if a board makes a decision that will have a substantial impact, board members may be unable to see the human implications of that decision because they're professionally distant—a strategy often masked as objectivity. When we operate from that place of distance, though, we are actually not being objective; instead, we are preventing ourselves from connecting using our intuitive brains, making it more difficult to get a sense of what matters to those around us.

I've seen this in action. About five years ago, I'd just finished a four-month tour around the world working with leadership teams from companies in Asia, Australia, Africa, the United States, and more. The Monday after I returned home to Holland, a colleague and I were in a facilitation meeting with the board of a Dutch insurance company. It was preparing for a large reorganization within its business. After running the numbers, it discovered that it miscalculated and that the endeavor would entail the letting go of more employees than it had originally intended. When that topic came up, the leaders discussed it in a way that, to me, felt dehumanizing—but not intentionally so. The leaders had no bad intent. On the whole, they were going through the motions, managing their business in a way that was ultimately in an effort to make things better. However, the level of detachment I witnessed in that meeting sent me into a sort of reverse culture shock, especially having traveled so extensively the months prior. I was not able to keep quiet in that moment, so I assisted the leaders in remembering that these were people's livelihoods at stake, not simply numbers on a spreadsheet. Their smirky laughs quieted, and we had a productive discussion that helped them remember the true picture. It was one they genuinely cared about, ultimately, but had lost sight of while trying to prioritize organizational efficiency *over and above* the human element, rather than *as a means to enhance it.*

The boards I mentioned, both the hypothetical and real, are examples that show that while the pain they may be inflicting through their company-wide decisions are not physical, it is present nonetheless. If Professional Closeness is not present, a level of detachment can permeate the perceptions of even the most well-intentioned leaders, and such decisions can simply be easier to make. **In the end, however, choices made without careful consideration of the human impact don't benefit the people or the overall organization, no matter what the numbers say.**

In addition, this way of operation is not how we are hardwired. Individuals will follow their own paths, whether implicitly or explicitly, around the deeper parts of their personalities: core values, basic temperament, and so forth. Professional Closeness is about translating those values and making them real through our own convictions, beliefs, and subsequent actions—and the consideration of the same in others. If we can accomplish this, not only will we be more personally productive, but our work environments will become more conducive to growth, too. Why? Just like the Milgram Experiments sought to explore, it all comes back to our nature and how we're designed to operate psychologically—topics I'll explore in depth very soon.

As the world becomes increasingly tech-driven, boards like the one I mentioned have myriad factors to consider when making decisions that will widely impact their organizations. **In these times, humans should become increasingly human again, not the other way around.**

OBEDIENCE TO AUTHORITY: MILGRAM'S RESEARCH AND PSYCHOLOGICAL DISTANCE

Yale psychologist Stanley Milgram was interested in Nuremberg war criminals' defenses for their horrific actions. In 1961, he designed and carried out an experiment to examine their justifications of "obedience." His aim was to explore how far humans would be influenced to go to harm others if instructed to do so by a perceived authority figure.

Milgram posted an advertisement for male subjects to participate in a (deceptively titled) "learning" experiment. His methodology then paired them up: one as a "learner" and the other a "teacher." This pairing up was rigged, however, so a study participant would always be allocated the teacher role. The learner, on the other hand, was always an actor or confederate, nicknamed "Mr. Wallace."

"Mr. Wallace," the learner, would sit alone in a separate room from the participant teacher, who sat in a lab. Also in the lab with an "experimenter," an authority figure—an electric shock generator that went from 15 V to a "severe" 450 V. With neither able to see the other, Mr. Wallace was given a selection of word pairs to learn before the teacher was told to test him. For each multiple-choice question Mr. Wallace answered incorrectly, the participant would shock him through the generator at increasingly higher voltages.

All participants went up to 300 V—after which Mr. Wallace began banging on the walls in pain—and 65 percent increased the voltage to a lethal 450 V. The most fascinating variation of this experiment in terms of professional distance was called the *Touch Proximity Condition*. When the participant teacher was no longer separate from Mr. Wallace, only 30 percent would administer a shock after 150 V.

THE OPPOSITE OF PROFESSIONAL DISTANCE

I've introduced the concept of professional distance, but here's a deeper analysis: the terminology actually stems from the medical field. In order to cope with the day-to-day and often emotionally heavy side effects of being a nurse or physician, the literature has historically argued (or at least implied) that detachment is necessary. By and large, caregivers are taught not to become too friendly with or emotionally attached to patients, as that may cloud judgment. As a result, many care providers take the role of "provider" more seriously than they do "care" in an emotional sense, relying more on expertise than connection.

In other words—and especially in the medical field—professionalism can often keep you from being close on a personal level, even though the level of connection we seek as humans can be similar. In these cases, we want the same level of trust and respect, but instead of saying, "be close," we say, "keep your distance."

However, 2008 empirical data published by Green and colleagues in the *Psychiatric Rehabilitation Journal* has shown that when patients truly feel their medical providers care about them, that has a direct, positive effect on their ability to heal. You can imagine why this dynamic is even more of a dilemma in this particular profession than it is in business; in medicine, you're quite literally dealing with life and death.

I believe, regardless of your profession, that expertise is important, but so is care. The two are not mutually exclusive, whether you're in a hospital or a boardroom. You don't have to exclude emotions entirely. In fact, it's the opposite: you should include them entirely. **Furthermore, leveraging emotional intelligence does not make you less objective; instead, it can help you see the whole of a person and the whole of a situation.**

Furthermore, I believe objectivity—in the medical profession or otherwise—is not something we should necessarily strive for, as subjectivity is part of human nature. There will always be something inherent about what you're interpreting, feeling, and assessing in any given scenario. Professional distance ignores it, and Professional Closeness leverages it. In fact, when it comes to leading your team, Professional Closeness is about creating the atmosphere within the group. This atmosphere allows you to start connecting people together and raising your collective intelligence—your inter-subjectivity—to ultimately become more rich and precise in your decision-making ability.

A LIVING CONCEPT IN ACTION

Professional Closeness, as a concept, is a living, breathing thing—much like the human beings who benefit from its implementation. The idea is still maturing as I write this book and use it in my practice; still, the empirical evidence of its effectiveness is clear.

Here's a tangible example: a couple of years ago, my consulting firm was working with a large, acquisition-based enterprise organization that had branches all over the globe. One business it acquired was a company founded in Thailand by two brothers. The brothers were proud and led their business with a distinct sense of control. They believed bosses needed to behave like bosses and employees needed to do what they were told, rather than criticize or bring different ideas to the table. The dynamic they created was clear-cut: leaders are active, and employees are passive.

My team was brought in to conduct a leadership program in which one brother—we'll call him Somchai—was a required participant. Others in the group belonged to the same, larger global conglomerate, so there were various cultures and senior levels of management experience represented in our group, too. We were warned outright: the regional HR director said Somchai would be "tough" to work with because he was a bit single-minded and arrogant at times.

"I'm curious as to how this is going to work," the HR director said to us. "I don't think your program is going to go over well with him."

Let's see, I thought. *We'll evaluate where we are after the week is over.*

We didn't brand the program as anything to do with Professional Closeness, although, looking back, it had many of the ingredients. Instead, it was a mix of leadership techniques, experiencing leading, being led, and self-discovery. We worked with our clients on skills like actively listening to those around them, tapping into the intelligence of their teams, and exploring the roots of certain not-so-functional behavioral patterns.

Much like the HR director predicted, Somchai did, indeed, have a challenging week. He was confronted on his beliefs and behaviors. Many in the group were on his same level professionally and managerially. As expected, Somchai exhibited a style of leadership he had learned and that he believed was right for the context. In other words, he was controlling and dominant; this attitude was completely unaccepted by his peers—many of whom were not shy about delivering feedback.

Somchai was shaken up, so I took the opportunity to connect with him. In fact, it wasn't hard to do—I could feel his struggle. He was acting the way his patterns were forcing him to, yet at the same time, he dared to recognize that another approach might work better. Still, making the change felt unfamiliar and even a little scary. I encouraged him to start small and experiment with little changes, even if that merely meant opening his mind and taking more time to listen rather than speak. As he made incremental progress, he gained confidence. By the end of the week, he was in no way completely changed, but his eyes were open.

A couple of months later, my team and I circled back to connect with the group and evaluated its progress. That same regional HR director who had warned us about Somchai initially now had a different response.

"I don't know what you guys did during training, but it

almost feels like he has taken a pill or something," she said. "The business is moving smoothly, and when we collaborate, it's constructive instead of an argument every time."

I understood what had happened, and there was no pill involved. Traditionally, Somchai had taken a distant role not because he was indeed arrogant but because the context under which he had been operating was blindingly linear: deliver, deliver, deliver. When he started to look at the world a different way—not a complete change, but even in small doses—he started to shift how he perceived his role and how he treated those around him. Not only was the feedback from the HR director positive on a personal level, but she indicated his new approach had a significant impact on the business as well.

What Somchai learned about the way he was facilitating himself and his team can also be used as a model for how you lead your organization today. **Think about the term "human resources" and what that means to you: if you look at your team members as resources, you get resources. If you look at them as humans, you get so much more.**

A REWARDING CHANGE

High achievers like Somchai can get a dopamine kick

when they hit their numbers, land a big contract, or make a sale. That fix, however, is a temporary one. When you start to operate from a place of Professional Closeness, you can experience a similar level of satisfaction that is far more long-lasting and rewarding: serotonin is released when you feel proud, when you connect with others, and when you achieve as a collective. In short, both feel good: you get a dopamine kick when you achieve on your own, but serotonin can only be gained in a group or social context—making it all the more important.

When you let Professional Closeness in, the way you relate to others will improve, and the way you handle conflict will be more effective. You can be more personally productive because you're better leveraging the talents and skills of those around you instead of keeping your head down, shouldering too much on your own. This dynamic creates a sense of belonging—almost a sense of family—where you can build and strive together.

WHAT'S NEXT?

In the following chapters, you'll find a deep discussion of how Professional Closeness impacts human relationships and, ultimately, business outcomes. Before we can understand how we show up in these organizational relationships, though, we must first understand what drives our human behavior in the first place: our brains. This cognitive exploration will give you the background information you need to be able to think deeply about not only your interactions and leadership style but also the way you move through the world as a person. In Chapter Two, we'll explore how what we know about neuroscience, instincts, and the laws of influence can help us better understand ourselves and others.

NATURE VS. NURTURE: THE PROFESSIONAL EDITION

How much of our behavior is driven by the makeup of our brains, and how much is context? What about instinct? What role does that play? We know much more about the answers to these questions today than we did twenty-five years ago, when neuroscience was relatively crude and unsophisticated. One thing is certain: evolutionary psychology says we are social animals, and we have three layers of our brains that perform different roles related to how we move through the world.

BRAIN BASICS

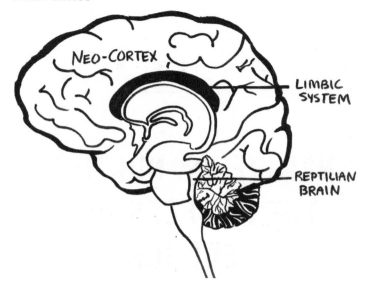

The layers of the brain also reflect the history of the earth, so to speak. The oldest part, known as the "crocodile" or reptilian brain (or the brain stem and core), is responsible for processing all sensory input, essentially acting as old-fashioned radar. This part of the brain is not able to define what is happening but rather reacts to assess basic questions like "Is this good or bad?" or "Is this safe or not?"

Around the crude structure of the reptilian brain is the mammalian brain, or the limbic brain. It also has to do with survival—but this time, survival in a group. This layer helps ensure you can read emotions. For example, if you walk into a room and immediately get a sense of tension or can pinpoint a hierarchy simply from social cues, that's your limbic brain in action.

Only in the last five million years, the neocortex—the largest and youngest part of the brain—began to evolve. The neocortex is responsible for so much: language, culture, creativity, analytical thought—essentially, what we perceive as those components that make us individuals.

Why is it important to understand these brain basics? **It's simple: what you feel is driving the bulk of your behavior—the neocortex, based on the discussion above—is not.** Experts in the field used to say, "the neocortex makes us human," but we now know most of our behavior is driven by the older parts of the brain—the reptilian and mammalian brains. We are hardwired for survival, individually and in groups. The neocortex comes in and creates a story—a context—based on what has *already been decided* by the two oldest parts of the brain. They act and react much faster, striving to ascertain "good or bad" and "safe or not"—high emotion decisions—long before the neocortex is able to consciously or unconsciously process a situation.

Here's how this relates to you as a leader. There's a common assumption some people have about business—especially in data-driven fields—that when people talk to one another, we're looking at the same shared, metaphorical screen. That way, we have a clear, identical point of reference. Then the outcome is purely logical, right? Wrong. If that were actually the case, all communication would be clear and linear—and, as we know, it's not. Why? As soon as people start to communicate, even if they're looking at the same data set, the oldest parts of the brain are hard at work, looking for signals: *Am I safe? What is my position in this group? Can I trust this person?*

Once you understand the interplay that goes on below the surface, you can look at your behavior in groups or teams—or the behavior of others with whom you regularly work—and see a new set of social factors unfolding beneath your day-to-day interactions.

INSTINCTS: WHAT YOU NEED TO KNOW

Evolutionary psychology argues, "You can take the man out of the Stone Age, but you can't take the Stone Age out of the man." This is a clever way of making a simple point:

the same types of behaviors are hardwired into everyone—instincts—and the biggest change has been context. In our lives today, many of these instincts or impulses are not relevant anymore. But, because evolution is not that fast, those behaviors are still there. Consider that the brain has evolved over 100 million years, but we only started living in cities about 10,000 years ago. All in all, it hasn't been that long that we've been working in what we know as modern-day organizations. We now know that the Dutch East India Company, which controlled the trade route from Europe to Asia, was the first organization to operate like a modern, global company—in 1602. Put into a twenty-four-hour clock, this means humans have only spent a couple of seconds working in what we consider "modern" organizations.

Let's explore a few of these hardwired instincts and how they relate to our exploration of ourselves, our teams, and Professional Closeness. Remember, these are not reactions we choose, yet they all play a role in some form in our day-to-day interactions.

As humans, we are innately averse to losing what we have. For instance, when you acquire something you've either paid for or gone through some trouble to get, it becomes inherently more valuable to you. Letting it go, even if the item itself is inconsequential in the grand scheme of things, can feel inexplicably difficult to do. It's no accident: imagine if you were alive 50,000 years ago, walking on the plain, and you found a bone. Perhaps you could use it as a tool. It could help you hunt or pry for the roots of whatever plant you were looking for. That tool was a deciding factor in whether you lived or died. Once you had it, you didn't want to let it go. Our brains internalized this message: "If you have something, hold on."

The effort we invest in acquiring the tool—which, by today's standards, could be a possession, a title, an idea, and so forth—plays a role in the value we assign to it. This is the reason IKEA is such a successful home furnishing company; when we put extreme effort into building something—and we own it—it becomes more valuable by default. It's also one reason people hold on to underperforming stocks. Even when they know they should sell, they think, "I'll hold on just a little bit longer." It's why some people hold on to jobs they hate; unconsciously, they know they've invested so much, and they're not willing to give up.

Our loss aversion instinct is evident in the business world, too. Every time you hear, "We need to change, reorganize, or adapt," you wake the crocodile. Your brain reacts. It wonders, *what am I going to lose?* **Studies have shown that when your amygdala or crocodile is rattled, you're largely unable to think logically or creatively anymore.** This is one reason we've been conditioned to "count to ten" or "take a deep breath" when triggered—to quiet the crocodile. This is to give us a chance to overcome our primal instinct, or at least see around the corner from it. Yet, to be honest—and also in my personal experience—it takes much longer to calm down an aroused crocodile. Until then, as you may already know, it's hard to think logically.

EMOTIONS BEFORE REASON

Recall that the emotional layer of the brain works much faster than the logical, cognitive layer. For that reason, emotion always comes first on the scope of human reactions. It's subconscious. **You can explain something in a logical and reasonable manner, but if you've awakened the emotional component in someone, the door to reason is closed. Or at best, access is delayed. Simple as that.** The brain is hardwired such that if anything is vague or ambiguous—anything other than 100 percent clear—our potential-danger and emotion-heavy red flags go off.

For example, imagine I'm the CEO of a company, and I know the results of the most recent quarter are a bit off-target. Suddenly, I receive a call on my cell phone from the chairman of the board. I stare at the ringing phone in my hand, and my immediate reaction—having no context whatsoever about what he is truly calling about—is rooted in emotion: *shit*, I think, *this is bad.*

BETTER SAFE THAN SORRY

The "emotions before reason" instinct is similar to the "better safe than sorry" instinct. Where does this come from? For example, say you're a VP leading a business unit of a well-established tech firm. A headhunter approaches you with a job offer that fully fits your ambitions. Yet the company is a startup that has been sending out some quite ambiguous signals on social media. You have two choices: first, jump at the opportunity, thinking you will have your dream job. Or, you can exercise caution and stay where you are. What do you do? For many of us, when the signals are vague, we err on the side of caution. Why? Back then, it was so you didn't die. Today, that self-preservation instinct still lives in us all.

Consider the news cycle for a moment: many people are more interested in learning about negative news than positive news, whether they admit it or not. Why? **Positive news is nice to hear, but it's not directly connected to survival.** If an area you're traveling to is facing a flood, however, you need to know so you can choose a different route—so you can live. If there's a heartwarming story, you'll read it if you have time, but it's not as much of a priority.

DO WE HAVE REPTILE BRAINS?

In 1977, Carl Sagan published a book called *The Dragons of Eden*. While the astronomer's book would win a Pulitzer the next year, the evolutionary neural theory that it brought to wider attention was developed by Dr. Paul MacLean during the 1960s. It premised that humans possess a three-in-one brain structure that evolved as layers over time, and arose from MacLean's EEG studies of patients with psychological disorders.

MacLean's Triune Brain Theory saw the brain's core and brainstem as the reptile brain, responsible for fight-or-flight and survival instincts. As time passed, he believed, the deep-rooted limbic system evolved around this as a second layer. This mammalian brain was responsible for emotions and our survival in group contexts. The youngest layer to evolve was the neocortex. Wrapped around the limbic system, to put it roughly, this most cognitively sophisticated layer governed rational, analytical, and "higher" thought.

The Triune Brain in Evolution (1990) was MacLean's seminal work, in which he drew on anatomical research into mammalian and reptile brains to develop his theory. While affective neuroscience has since discredited his theory of the brain's evolving in layers over time, it remains heavily influential thanks to its highly effective explanation of higher (and "lower") brain functions in emotional behavior. With this understanding, it is argued that we can better come to comprehend the different—and often conflicting—instincts that influence our leadership behavior.

LEADERSHIP AND STATUS

The aforementioned three instincts—loss aversion, emotions before reason, and better safe than sorry—all stem from our reptilian brain. It makes sense, after all, as they're rooted in sheer survival.

Our leadership and status instinct, however, comes from the limbic part of the brain. As humans, we are constantly—whether consciously or subconsciously—trying to determine status. Why? From an evolutionary standpoint, the lower you are in the pecking order, the worse off you are. Today, we strive to connect with those who have a higher status, all the while trying to ascertain who we are to the rest of our given group. Our instinct is to ask ourselves, *where do we fit in? Who is in the lead?*

This is why many young professionals aim to ascend the ranks or become a manager—often, for the wrong reasons. They want the status that comes with the job; it's simply how we're hardwired. This quest for status is even true in group situations where everyone is on a "level playing field." When the straightforward status indicators are not applicable—ladder climbing, higher titles, etc.—people find other ways to show where they stand. They may turn to name-dropping, for example, to raise their perceived position among their peers.

SOCIAL CHITCHAT OR SOCIAL GROOMING

Chimps connect by looking for fleas in the fur of other chimps. It's a bonding process. In our evolution, as people have become people, we are no longer looking for fleas in each other's fur. Instead, we are doing something similar—chitchatting or gossiping, another instinct from the mammalian layer of our brains. For our purposes, this means exchanging what is, on the outside, seemingly unimportant information—but that seemingly unimportant information gives you insight into the subtler social dynamics playing out within the social group.

Knowing your status in the group and having a penchant for gossip are connected instincts. For example, in an organizational setting, it's inherently known that if you truly want something to be spread around the office, it's best to communicate it in an informal manner. Then you can be sure everyone will get wind of it. **In other words, as soon as something becomes gossip, people remember—even if your official and unofficial communications have very similar content.** It's simply how we're wired.

RECOGNIZE AND DEFEAT DEFENSIVENESS

The suggested layering of the brain and our instinctual reactions to stimuli can manifest physically and psychologically as defensiveness. When you're under pressure or have a feeling of being unsafe, your body reacts: perhaps your temperature starts to rise, or maybe your skin becomes clammy. The speed of your speech may increase, and you may feel tightness in your chest or stomach. There's a bit of fight or flight at play here, too; maybe you feel caught in the headlights, maybe you leave the interaction as quickly as possible, or maybe you become too emotionally attached and escalate to a point that doesn't serve you well in the moment.

When this happens, it's important to understand that being defensive—however it looks for you—is not your fault; it's a product of how our brain is structured. Still, this reaction is not in any way helping you. The good news is that once you understand how defensiveness originates within and affects you—partly by looking for triggers and partly by understanding your biological instincts—you can choose to react in a different way. This is not to say you'll be able to eliminate the reaction entirely, but getting a handle on it gives you an extreme advantage when it comes to interacting with others and letting your emotions work for you, not against you.

Consider Ella, for example. She led a large unit in an enterprise organization, and she had the tendency to be highly reactive—strong, coarse, crude, and overruling. In other words, her crocodile snapped loudly and often. In fact, it did more than snap; it attacked, and that left others in her organization laying low and trying not to provoke the reptile. Ella's approach was rooted in a type of defensiveness stemming from slivers of all the instincts we've discussed, and she forced those she led into a permanent state of passiveness. In short, nobody wanted to deal with Ella, but everybody had to. The dynamic created so much tension in the organization that it caught the CEO's attention, and he then gave Ella one chance to get her act together.

My team had the opportunity to coach Ella, and we showed her there were other ways to process her defensiveness. It took time, though. Her first reaction was—not surprisingly—defensive: "Sorry, this is just me. I will never be able to listen better. It's not who I am," she said. She may have quit if not for the ultimatum given to her by the CEO: "Change (with our support), or go."

After two sessions, it became easier for Ella to give herself the opportunity to change. She let go of the snap to loss aversion—in this case, the fear of losing the identity to which she so closely adhered—and discovered she could change her self-image for the better. In turn, she learned that she could positively affect others. After a few more sessions, Ella learned her team was smarter and more creative than she had originally given it credit for. It took time, but she was eventually able to reroute her reactions.

Six months later, Ella was liked and respected by her colleagues and coworkers. She was still delivering results, but now she was doing so in an atmosphere that fostered growth. Of course, she reportedly can still be snappy at times—you can't change your hardwiring completely—but the difference, as reported by the CEO, has been night and day.

WHAT'S NEXT?

Everything I've discussed in this chapter—the layers of the brain, instincts, and understanding defensiveness—is to open your eyes to the fact that we are so much more driven by our primal instincts and emotions than we give credit to in our rational, day-to-day realities. If we can begin to deepen our awareness of why we do what we do—and why others do what they do—we can step closer into the power of Professional Closeness and improve our outcomes.

In the next chapter, we'll explore how to leverage this newfound (or maybe found again) knowledge into breaking down silos in your business—and why that's incredibly important on the path to meaningful and measurable growth.

CHAPTER THREE

THE VALUE OF INTERCONNECTIVITY: BREAKING DOWN SILOS

I got the call four weeks before the important meeting was to begin—a gathering of thirty-five top-level managers from all over the world, all from different departments, coming together to discuss collective enterprise strategy. Eight months of preparation, including several workshops, had preceded this meeting, and now they were scrambling. Communication had broken down. People were either negative to one another or not speaking at all. They needed a professional facilitator, or all the resources and time they'd dedicated to the meeting would go to waste.

"Do you have time for an urgent assignment?" the voice

on the other end of the line asked. "I understand if you don't, given that you might be going on summer holiday. But if you do, we could really use you. Oh, and by the way—the meeting is in India."

I was intrigued. I had planned free time but no vacation plans yet, and it sounded like I was needed. I ran it by my girlfriend, and we both agreed I should take the job. That's not to say I wasn't hesitant: in my line of work, I've found that people in high positions generally have big egos. I wondered in earnest if the situation was already too far deteriorated. Still, I put together a program and went on my way.

When I arrived, I found the situation dire. Everyone had come together with a common objective, but they had no process for achieving it. Leaders were the definition of siloed, focusing only on their own interests. **Each person was trying to maximize their personal gains instead of looking at the collective interests of the business. Everyone was on their own island, and there were no ferries moving among them.**

Basically, they were wasting their time.

The first step I took was so simple, yet so necessary: I had to get the leaders to remember that they were all people. Because "reptilian" thinking had led to silo mentalities in the first place, it was time for other brain areas to step up. I had them look at each other from a human perspective, instead of simply from the functions or departments each represented. I helped them focus on their relationships first—nothing about their business objectives or the mission of the meeting. That meant getting them to think more with their mammalian brains, to realize that to work together, we need to see ourselves as part of something bigger.

That took time, but it worked.

Once humanity started to settle in the room again, negativity lessened. People started to relax. Then I gradually helped them take a step back: What were they here to discuss? What information did they already have, and how could they look at it differently? We spent time organizing data and having real, open discussions. I dared them to go back and reconsider previous positions, seeing if perhaps the pieces of the puzzle might fit together a bit differently to arrive at a better outcome. In a sense, we worked retroactively, starting at square one. The approach created clarity and social energy in the room instead of ambiguity and standoffishness.

By the time we got to the end of the four-day session, the atmosphere in the group had changed from one of hopelessness and negativity to one of relief. The ferries were moving again. The leaders still didn't always agree, but they could communicate and open their minds to solutions that would serve the objective, not just themselves. By leveraging Professional Closeness, I was able to bring them back to the state of mind from which true collaboration is possible: people are people, and if we approach them with openness, humility, and modesty, we can move forward together, unsiloed.

DEFRAGMENTATION: WHAT YOU NEED TO KNOW

The term "breaking down silos" has become a bit of a buzzword, much like being a "disruptor" in business today. Let's take the buzz out of the equation, for a moment, and examine what silos truly are, how they got here, and why you should work to eliminate them in your organization. One way to look at this is through the lens of defragmentation.

Consider what happens when you defragment your hard drive: initially, when your drive is still fragmented, the disk starts to organize information into allocated spots. However, they're not neatly organized; they're just that: open spots. Your hard drive is then full of bits and pieces of information. The defragmentation process frees up space on the disk, organizing the information in the correct way.

This concept has been applied in the business world, too.

Many organizations are built on Scientific Management principles, which come from the early Industrial Revolution. It makes sense that in a manufacturing-heavy environment, cutting processes into many tiny pieces is a productive strategy. That has evolved: over time, the specialization of those functions and tasks has been translated into the specialization of departments. Today, we have entire organizations that are basically compilations of these special functions—or silos. Proponents believe this strategy still leads to increased productivity, but what I actually see nowadays is different: due to technological innovations such as cloud computing and other communication and automation technologies, we've got more opportunities to connect than ever before. The mindset of "the more specialized you are, the more productive you become" no longer holds water.

At some point, organizations need to come together to heal themselves. When their internal hard drives are all over the place—fragmented, disjointed, and scrambled—it is necessary to reset. To defragment—not in a way that creates further silos, but in a way that creates space, organizes information, and builds bridges to make the organization whole again.

This is not to say your business cannot have specialized units anymore—far from it. Your team members do what they do for a reason: because they're good at it. You would not break down the accounting side of your business and ask marketers to fill out tax forms, for example. **The difference is in the _connectivity_ among different departments, not their skillsets.**

Defragmentation to make your company whole again is about the synapses between silos and the interplay between departments. Think about your organization as a neural network: the reptilian, mammalian, and neocortex all have different functions, but the magic is in how they work together. The same can be true for what you once considered silos. **Ask yourself: How can you make more energetic and lively connections among your teams? Resist the urge to jump straight into a reorganization—which, much of the time, simply leads to different silos.** Instead, think of your business like a series of electrical circuits: focus less on the two ends of the connection, and more on the connection itself.

THE FALL OF SCIENTIFIC MANAGEMENT

The end of the Civil War heralded an explosion of industrialization across America. As the productivity power of machines became ever more apparent, more focus—and managerial frustration—began shifting toward the workers who ran them. Seemingly the weak link or bottleneck on the path to larger and larger scale production, aggrieved business owners started looking for ways their workers could reach maximum efficiency.

In the hub of this, engineer and former machine shop laborer Frederick Taylor initiated what he called "time studies" at the steel plant where he worked. Armed with a stopwatch, he would strip down and segment different tasks that the workers carried out, measure how long they took to the nearest ten milliseconds, and attempt to determine the most efficient way to do them. Taylor took on the study of tasks as segmented as shoveling and iron-handling later and refined his task-breakdown approach into what he termed Scientific Management, sometimes now referred to as Taylorism.

While Taylor's approach to management was arguably about making workers' lives easier, it begs a bigger question for organizations today. That is, if human systems are discretely segmented into specialized tasks—even micro-tasks—who has ownership of the final output? Where does intrinsic motivation come into processes that are fragmented into component parts, and where is the cohesion—the connection—that makes us better together?

SILOS FALL: CASE STUDY

Once, my colleague Marc and I worked with an established company that sought to expand into different markets and geographies to meet shareholder needs. It hired a new CEO, and the CEO put together a highly competent team to help the company move forward. When we came into the picture, it'd done a lot of great work and had just begun to establish its presence in their third new market—no small feat.

There was a problem, though: their work all depended on the strength and competence of the individual members of the group. The CEO admitted he had forgotten one thing: he told me he'd recruited everyone from an individual skills perspective, but he'd neglected to make sure they could act as one. In expanding into those initial new markets, his team had moved mountains. He had great respect for the team. At that point, though, the lack of a common objective among the group was causing the company challenges. The CEO, while pleased with the growth of the organization, was trying to take the company to the next stage. He knew the company needed a change in dynamic.

When we met with the group, the severity of those challenges came into light. We asked what was missing, and the word "trust" came up more than once. Note that this was not a deep, human-level mistrust of one another in a "backstabbing" way; rather, it was a superficial mistrust. Could each high performer trust the other high performers to deliver what they promised? Would it be on time and done well? Each leader had a specific skill, and they focused only on delivering their piece into the collective. The collective itself, however, was not top of mind. The connections among team members were so weak that there wasn't even a sense of common accomplishment; they focused only on meeting individual goals.

Over a number of months, we worked with the group. We helped it build a common sense of belonging and purpose while still giving members the space to excel individually and celebrate their unique accomplishments. Together, as we unsiloed their attitudes and homed in on those connections, the energy within the group shifted. In the end, the team was able to look back and not only celebrate what it'd achieved together but also question how much further it could have gone had it been functioning as a unit from the beginning.

WHAT'S NEXT?

Did the group of high performers we just discussed have skill? Absolutely. Did they have an organizational culture that supported them? Absolutely not. To the CEO's credit, he recognized that and made the correction.

Peter Drucker famously wrote, "Culture eats strategy for breakfast." I argue that both are true. In an unsiloed environment—moreover, a holistic environment, which we'll cover in-depth in Part II of this book—culture *meets* strategy for breakfast. In the end, breakfast is breakfast, and success is success—but, like most things, they're both better when shared.

PART II

PUTTING IT INTO PRACTICE: IMPLEMENTING A HOLISTIC APPROACH

CHAPTER FOUR

LEARN FROM THE FUTURE AND USE COLLECTIVE INTELLIGENCE

Would you step into a car and start driving if you had a blacked-out windshield? What if you could only look in your rearview mirror while trying to move forward? How long do you think you'd be able to survive that ride?

The answer is obvious, yet that's how many organizations approach growth today. It's always appeared strange to me how companies put so much emphasis on past performance, under the assumption that a close examination of what's worked before will continue to be successful in the future. You can learn from the past, but repeating it blindly and being unwilling to pivot is *not* a surefire way to move forward—no matter how many metrics you examine or KPIs you set. A better approach is to learn from the future. Let's explore.

EXPLOITATION AND EXPLORATION

Exploitation in the business sense is what you already do well. It's about leveraging your strengths to stay efficient and profitable, regardless of your industry. In other words, it's the heart of business as we know it. Exploration, on the other hand, is exactly what it sounds like: trying to branch out and looking for new opportunities that safeguard your profitability and relevance not just today, but tomorrow.

Each approach requires a different mindset. If you're exploitation-focused, for example, you have a high level of trust in what has worked before. The problem comes when you try to apply those strategies moving forward without exploring the path ahead; you could very well be driving toward a cliff and not know it. What if the market shifts? What if the road ends?

That's what happened to Kodak—but you already knew that. What you may *not* know, though, is the whole story.

The story of Kodak's failure to pivot appropriately—its emphasis on the rearview mirror and exploitation over exploration—is old news. An interesting component of the story, though, is the trajectory of Kodak's next-in-line rival, Fujifilm. Let's start from the beginning: Kodak made its money from the production of film and photo paper. Faced with the fact that the world was becoming more and more digital, it was also actually one of the first companies to develop digital photography—but it ignored it. It had a highly profitable healthcare imaging branch, too, but it sold it. Why? Kodak was not, as some report, change-averse, however—it just chose the wrong change. Aware that the market was being disrupted and hoping to get ahead of it, the company installed 10,000 digital kiosks in Kodak partner stores, attempting to apply its same business model to the new market.

For over forty years, Fuji trailed Kodak as the market leader in the space. It was used to exploration; it had to be for survival. When Kodak began to show signs of trouble, Fuji looked through the windshield and was able to see the bridge was giving out on the way people historically consumed its products. What did it do? It looked at what other technologies it had and what they could potentially mean for other markets in the future. For example, Fujifilm recognized that certain chemicals helped printed photos keep their color longer, and it found a way to repurpose that technology into a line of cosmetics products that helped protect skin from discoloring or sagging. Fujifilm also applied its light technology to the polarization of LCD screens, which was wildly successful as well.

In the end, both Kodak and Fuji looked at the same problem through different lenses, and they both aimed to change. One lens was slanted too far to the past, and the other to the future. History has decided the winner.

LEARNING FROM THE FUTURE IN ACTION: FULL SPEED AHEAD

One of my clients is a highly successful global company that has been in business for over fifty years. Recently, however, the leaders felt the organization "business as usual" was beginning to reach its expiration date for effectiveness. The market was shifting, and they were paying attention. Still, they proposed initiative after initiative that mirrored Kodak's kiosk flop: looking ahead, but from the same perspective. They called us in to help.

The executives knew they had to approach whatever their next move would be from a future-oriented mindset, yet doing so was far from intuitive. In fact, the process was painful, as some leaders bucked at the thought of what they perceived as "losing" what had long been core to their business. For a few, it was as if they didn't recognize themselves anymore as entrepreneurs. For some, they found it hard to justify spending money on ideas that may or may not come to fruition. Others felt it was a waste of time. The battle between short- and long-term thinking was real, and rightfully so. After all, business is about generating outcomes, and when you don't know whether or not you'll have a positive return on your investment—i.e., the backbone of learning from the future—taking steps in a new direction can feel risky and even antithetical to what you've been taught. All these points are valid: putting thirty to forty highly paid managers into one room and dedicating substantial time and energy not to creating or selling, but to ideating? That's a hard pill to swallow.

Those who swallowed it and stayed, however—and those who eventually changed their tunes and came back—were dedicated to focusing on the firm's potential, not its past. They created an approach that allocated and dedicated a substantial amount of the company's time to exploration and search while at the same time defining solutions focused on exploitation. Practically, they gathered leaders from across their value chain who had perspectives relevant to the task at hand, and asked key questions: What will our consumers want the day after tomorrow? Who will our consumers be in ten years? What can we do to meet them there?

Today, their outlook on the future business potential has tripled, backed up by validated and identified new opportunities. And they're starting to see real money come from the fruits of the time, energy, and resources they invested in exploration. They continue to successfully challenge their basic assumptions about their business, which has taken substantial guts. It has been my pleasure and honor to support and facilitate this group.

BUT WHAT ABOUT DATA?

At this point, it's important to note that exploration doesn't mean abandoning hard facts. But data, by definition, describes what has already occurred. After all, that's how the data was generated in the first place. And of course, there are also scores of data that, when leveraged into predictive models, can help leaders see around corners. I imagine, for example, that both Kodak and Fuji had the same data about consumer trends surrounding photo printing. My argument is that it's how they used that data—and what they combined it with—that matters.

When aiming to run your organization holistically, it's important to tread lightly here. Why? Data is essential to progress, and I would never dispute that. It can answer innumerable questions for the exploitative side of your business; that's all true. When it comes to the explorative side of your business, though—when answering questions like who your new customers will be or what the next big industry shift holds—you'll simply never have foolproof data. Thinking you will is a trap. The way out of that trap requires a combination of examining the data and using collective intelligence.

THE FUTURE OF WORK

As blockchain technology becomes incrementally more accessible in a mainstream sense, we are seeing collective intelligence, or "Superminds," at work on a much greater scale. Distributed Ledger Technology—a consensually shared database with no sole administrator—is an example of how a specific goal—trading assets—has been streamlined by numerous humans at work together in a specialized environment.

However, our emotional reptile and mammal brains are activated so instantly by the threat of "technological unemployment," as Keynes put it, that we tend to overlook the ways in which collective intelligence sets us apart from machines. The best possible parallel I can make at this point in our technological evolution is with strategic planning. While AI is algorithmically capable of generating myriad potential futures, it is still much quicker, easier, and—most importantly—meaningful to do so as a group of humans.

When it comes to shaping the changes that we want to see, culture is always much more powerful than strategy. The social, human elements of a group are what allow us to make and share tools like AI, but they're also how we decide whether that's something we want to do in the first place. Intuition and being in touch with our emotions as a collective lets us look into the unknown together and think holistically rather than just as a sum of analytical parts—much like I recommend leaders do within their organizations.

COLLECTIVE INTELLIGENCE: WHAT IT IS AND WHY IT MATTERS

Collective intelligence is not as simple as gathering many smart people in a room. I've shared multiple examples already of teams of incredibly talented leaders who found themselves at stagnation points. Why? Was it because they weren't intelligent? The answer is no: it's because they weren't intelligent *as a unit*. I define collective intelligence as it relates to companies as the way in which you combine and optimize the individual thinking power of people—not just executives—in order to solve an organizational problem or meet a collective objective.

It's natural to think that if you create a safe environment where team members feel comfortable, respected, and satisfied, it will raise the collective intelligence of that group by default. As it turns out, that's not the case. Thomas Malone, an MIT professor, recently wrote *Superminds*, a book that—among other things—covers three factors proven to do just that:

1. **Social perceptiveness.** Social perceptiveness is the level at which individual members of a group can read others' mental states. For example, do they pay attention to body language? Facial expressions? The higher the group members' social perceptiveness, the higher the group's collective intelligence—a correlation that fits with what we know to be true of the limbic system.

2. **The degree of equality in participation.** This factor is connected to both the limbic part of the brain and the neocortex because it has a social component and an empathetic component. When those in a group can put themselves in the shoes of others—i.e., show empathy—there tends to be more equal participation and more effective communication. Groups with one or two people who command or hog the conversation have a lesser degree of collective intelligence than those where multiple people not only speak but actively listen. Even if they're the smartest people in the room.

3. **The number of women in the group.** In his research, Malone found that the higher the number of women in a group, the higher its collective intelligence. This is a combination of factors one and two, as women biologically have higher levels of social perceptiveness and empathy.

At this juncture, it's important not to conflate collective intelligence with Professional Closeness too much. A group of people who leverage Professional Closeness are, by definition, going to score higher on points one and two from Malone's research. That does not mean, though, that these teams are in close physical proximity or are best friends outside of work. Professional Closeness, remember, is rooted in respect and understanding—not necessarily friendship.

But that doesn't mean your group can't share a pizza or two. Let me explain.

COLLECTIVE INTELLIGENCE IN ACTION: THE GOOD, THE BAD, AND THE UGLY

Online retail empire Amazon is an example of an organization that leverages collective intelligence well. The company has instituted what it calls the two-pizza rule: if a group or team is too large to feed with two pizzas, it's too large to be effective. Why? Think back to Malone's points one and two: the more people in a room, the harder it is to be socially perceptive, and the harder it is to ensure everyone has optimal speaking time. Amazon's two-pizza teams make decisions autonomously; in other words, they're trusted. Then they connect with other teams to share the decisions and build from there instead of starting each meeting from square one. At Amazon, teams dissolve, reform, and share insights and decisions all the time in order to best meet the objective at hand. If a team isn't successful, there isn't infighting; the team disbands, and members form a new one.

The way Amazon approaches decision making—with a quasi-neural network of small teams working autonomously yet in a highly connected fashion—allows it to stay agile and innovative. It's no coincidence that the benefits of decentralized decision making—motivation, creativity, and flexibility—are some of the success factors of modern businesses.

On the other hand, consider banks during the financial crisis of 2008. Some went bankrupt, some escaped and managed to hold on, and others were able to thrive again. What can we learn? Banks that did not fare well had a semi-authoritarian style of leadership pre- and post-crash. Even if managers or other executives disagreed with a decision those above them in the company were suggesting, the environment was such that speaking out felt too much like a risk—a reaction rooted in our "better safe than sorry" instinct for survival. In the end, those banks had little to no collective intelligence, and they didn't make it.

When we examine these failed banks, it's interesting to note that before the financial crisis, those same organizations—with that same authoritarian leadership—weren't struggling. At least outwardly. Their lack of collective intelligence was bubbling under the surface, and it took an environmental trigger to cause the issues it created to come to light.

These make-or-break moments don't always come in the form of an economy-changing market crash; if your organization has low collective intelligence, any challenge or conflict—no matter how seemingly small—can turn into a much larger hurdle.

A TOOL—AND A COUNTERWEIGHT

Teams with higher collective intelligence achieve higher outputs, and—ironically, given the discussion of data earlier—this is not an empirical assumption; it's proven. You can use this information as an opportunity to review your own teams. For example, if you have a group of ten men making all the decisions, you will have better outcomes by including women in the group—a science-backed case for gender diversity in leadership. This isn't only about decision making, either: if you are striving to break down silos and approach your business more holistically, building your collective intelligence is a strong place to start.

GROUPTHINK: ON BANKS AND COLLECTIVE DELUSIONS

Quality decisions quite frequently take time and effort. Groupthink—where dysfunctional decisions go unchallenged—often arises and perseveres because we need to address certain criteria for collective intelligence. Arguably, it's not as easy as simply throwing people together for consensus or dictating with omniscience how things should go. One of the three collective intelligence conditions, *equal participation*, can be particularly crucial when the stakes are high and the instinct for loss aversion swells.

Research into groupthink during the 2008 financial crisis suggests that semi-autocratic leadership played a large contributing role in many poor decisions made prior to Lehman's collapse. Notably, some literature argues that groupthink was prevalent throughout numerous stages leading up to the crisis—starting with a willful collective blindness to growing warning signs and worsened by the discouragement of dissenters. Toward crunch time, Laurence Ball argues in *The Fed and Lehman Brothers,* unchallenged self-deception and optimism were especially influential in the decision for the bank to default. An unnecessary default, he premises.

All this speaks to the importance of connections between individuals and the need for leaders to foster a culture where collective intelligence can thrive. Without a culture where people feel safe to think critically, and are secure in speaking up, disconnected conformity can become the norm. As the banks showed us, unopposed over-optimism can trigger overly risky decisions, yet collective emphasis on loss aversion can have equally detrimental outcomes. It works both ways.

WHAT'S NEXT?

To propel your company forward, it seems fitting to examine what's been effective in the past. This is a sound strategy, but only when you learn from that examination, are willing to have an open mind, and can acknowledge any past mistakes. That is, it's important not to lean too heavily into the past and project those same strategies and perspectives in your next move. How can you see around the corner? **I have no magic bullet for you; it is challenging and sometimes scary to look into the unknown, but upping your team's collective intelligence and being open to new ideas are two ways to ensure you aren't ignoring the "washed-out road ahead" signs as you drive into the future.**

Operating from a place of Professional Closeness is paramount to running your business holistically, allowing you to heed those signs. A big part of doing so effectively seems basic, yet it's critical: you have to know who is in the car with you, and you have to know how to interact with them to get the best results.

In the next chapter, we'll explore the laws of influence and how you can master them to drive results.

CHAPTER FIVE

MASTER THE LAWS OF INFLUENCE

I was once tasked with facilitating a leadership meeting between two groups who spoke different languages—literally, not figuratively. We utilized robust language interpretation technology, and everyone wore headphones so spoken content was translated in the particular language each attendee could understand, all in real time. Initially, I was concerned they would have difficulty connecting.

I was wrong.

It was astonishing to watch them communicate on a nonverbal level. Despite what I perceived initially as a barrier, the energy in the room was high. It makes sense neurologically, as language is a function of the cognitive part of the brain. Connecting and relating, though, stem from the limbic part of the brain, which has no capacity for language. **This means that when we are communicating in close proximity, or even over video, we don't need words as much as we think we do to explain ourselves.** A big part of the reason why comes down to influence.

WHAT IS INFLUENCE?

Before we proceed, I must make a critical distinction regarding the definition of influence: it is very different from manipulation, which is getting another person or group of people to do what you want them to do. Influence is not selling. The truth is that you have influence in *every* interaction, whether you're conscious of it or not. For example, if you're active in a conversation and speaking dominantly, you have an influence on those listening because you're emanating an air of authority. If you're listening authentically and asking relevant questions, you're having an influence on the speaker because you're giving an air of engagement. If, in that same conversation, you're doing nothing and are completely checked out, you have an influence on everyone because you're giving an air of disinterest.

Whether you realize it or not, you're always creating an impact. So it's up to you to decide what impact you want to have.

THE LAWS OF INFLUENCE

In the 1950s, psychologist Timothy Leary developed a concept called the Rose of Leary that speaks to interactive behavior. Essentially, the concept states that when we interact with one another, we exert influence, whether consciously or subconsciously.

In my day-to-day reality as an organizational practitioner, I use a modern and much more accessible version of this concept: The "Sphere of Influence."* The SOI takes the best of Leary's rose and combines it with Simon Sinek's Golden Circle. It's a concept you can use to guide and help you in your interactions and observations. In addition, as a 360-feedback tool, you can use it to dissect individuals' preferred behavior styles and expose team dynamics.

There are two dimensions to the concept: a vertical axis that qualifies how much you are actively "leading" or "following" in an interaction and a horizontal axis that centers on your content- or relationship-orientation. (More on this in a moment.)

---

* See www.sphereofinfluence360.com.

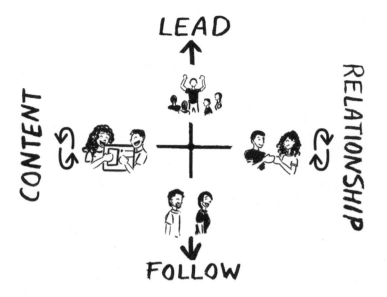

The vertical axis examines how you present yourself in the conversation, ranging from leading to following behavior. For example, are you talking a lot? Are you taking initiative? Or are you more of a listener and not as verbally present? One end of the spectrum is not better than the other; this is simply an evaluation of how we present ourselves.

Note, too, that whether you're active or passive is about much more than simply how much you're speaking; it's also connected to how powerful or powerless you feel in a given interaction. Again, where you fall on the spectrum at any one time affects those in the room, whether consciously or subconsciously. If you're exuding strength and speaking a lot, you're nudging others into a space of passivity. If you're timid or quiet, you're not only opening the door for someone else to be active—you're compelling them to. You've created a void in the interaction that psychologically must be filled.

Both active and passive roles must be filled for an interaction to be productive. If two leaders are active and dominant—that is, they bring the same level of energy to a conversation and are both apt to speak up—one must eventually take a more passive role in order for anything to get accomplished. This is not a negative or weak action; it is a choice. If neither makes it, the resulting dynamic might look like an interaction, but it is not one. Instead, in reality it will be a series of two monologues running simultaneously.

The horizontal axis in the Sphere of Influence examines what needs to be accomplished in the interaction. What are you talking about? What is on the table? From a relationship perspective, how relevant is the content to you as a person? How relevant is it to others in the room, and what are the commonalities?

THE BASICS

When I talk about the Sphere of Influence, I always say that the concept has a lot of details and dimensions, but what you really need to remember is very basic: the three key points of the Sphere of Influence are that, depending on where you fall on the spectrum, leading behavior from one person inherently triggers following behavior in others and vice versa. On the other side, however, opposite laws apply. Content-oriented behavior triggers content-oriented behavior, and relationship-oriented behavior triggers relationship-oriented behavior.

USING THE SPHERE OF INFLUENCE

What does this mean to you? If you understand the underlying triggers in all our interactions, you can approach a business situation proactively rather than reactively. For example, leaders often tend to think they need to be active in interactions because that's what is expected. They come into a situation with an attitude of "what's next," or sometimes with a "leading" mentality: "Don't talk to me about problems; just give me the solutions." This approach triggers passiveness in others. Team members who may be active and self-confident in other scenarios will hesitate to speak up and take ownership of their ideas. On the content side, if the discussion is solely around hitting numbers and driving results—with no care to the relationship side of the spectrum—the leader creates a pattern that inhibits growth in the organization and harms the potential for true collaboration.

The inverse is also true. It is possible to overemphasize

the relationship side of the spectrum such that it, too, inhibits measurable growth. For example, if a leader is strictly inspirational and focuses on the emotional impact/dynamics of an interaction, it's almost guaranteed nothing concrete will come of the meeting. This is especially true if their approach presents as overly active, triggering unintended passiveness in others. The effect is everybody feels warm and fuzzy but nothing gets done.

The concept has many layers and much more to it than I'll cover in this book. The bottom line, however, is simple: you need both. You need balance. Sometimes, leaders must actively lead; sometimes, they must listen. Some situations, too, will call for switching between the two as things play out. Sometimes, leaders must focus on content; sometimes, they must focus on relationships—again, both can happen within the space of one interaction. Acknowledging this need to adapt is one of the core elements of your ability to lead with emotions in mind and leverage Professional Closeness.

LAWS IN ACTION: WHAT CAN YOU LEARN?

Communication preferences and patterns as they relate to the laws of influence are determined early on when people meet. Even if you're in a large group and haven't known the others long, the influence people exude on one another can tell you where they fall in the Sphere.

And you, too, can understand the same about your own tendencies. It's interesting to examine how we modify our behavior accordingly. For example, if you know you're about to go into a meeting where the same three people speak 70 percent of the time, you're likely less apt to bring ideas to that interaction. Conversely, if you're one of the ones speaking 70 percent of the time, you're likely less apt to listen should someone break the pattern. It's important to note that's exactly what it is: a pattern—and a hard one to change if you're not conscious of it.

Change is difficult, but not impossible. Once you know your preference and the preferences of those you're communicating with, you can modify your behavior accordingly by weighing it against its potential impact. Sometimes, a CEO running a meeting solo is a necessary part of business. Sometimes, a lower-ranking team member has an idea or thought that could add value to the meeting. If neither is willing to consciously break their pattern, nobody wins.

In my work with clients, I've generally found it to be true that the higher your position in the pecking order, the more conscious you should be about letting others speak. Take the ego out. Or at least suspend your ego.

INFLUENCING VS. PERSUADING AS A LEADER

Leading is not persuading—it is influencing, and it is listening. It is authentically being interested in what others have to say, where they come from, and what makes them tick. It is knowing who is in the room—where they fall on the active/passive spectrum and how their natural communication tendencies manifest.

You may think, "I've worked hard to be the CEO. I didn't do that to *not* persuade others and be in charge of meetings." That, however, is the wrong attitude, especially if you are striving for collective intelligence. As you'll recall, social perceptiveness is a key element of collective intelligence. **Noticing imbalance in interactions is important, and it's why, at times, great leaders make themselves small on purpose. In specific, highly relevant contexts, they make themselves big.** Succinctly, great leaders know the difference between persuading and influencing.

This is not to say that leadership doesn't come with a strong sense of ownership over interactions. The CEO, for example, owns the outcome of a meeting more than the six other directors in the room with her. To lead effectively, the CEO must clearly assess what she needs to happen as a result of the interaction—i.e., the content. What decision needs to be made? What is the goal of the meeting? Once she has a clear understanding of the intended result, she can retrofit her approach to attaining it. Not in a manipulative way but in a way that genuinely prioritizes the organization's success and empowers her team in the process.

This step seems simple conceptually, but it can be challenging in practice. In fact, one of the biggest challenges I find organizations facing is that leaders fail to focus on the real outcome and instead devote too much energy on the activities that lead to the outcome. They get bogged down with milestones, incremental tasks, and so forth. **When micromanagement clouds good leadership, even once-strong leaders lose sight of the big picture. In these scenarios, people generally feel controlled and unmotivated. Often, this isn't a sign of a poor leader; it's a sign of poor focus.** On the other hand, leaders who remain open, communicative, and focused on the larger outcome generate the opposite response: team members are engaged and on board.

TEAMWORK STYLES IN ACTION

Insights from the Sphere of Influence can also be helpful in understanding our teams. In collaborative situations, we're often inclined to bring a broader "quadrant" of styles to the table—we can think of these as the different emphases we place on content and relationships when working together. Given that our approaches can either discourage or encourage others to respond in certain ways, things naturally get more dynamic.

But you don't need to be a longtime facilitator to leverage the knowledge that diverse influencing styles can both clash with and complement one another. When one team member is quiet and focused on details, for instance, this creates even more space for an already fairly dominant colleague to lead. It's why self-awareness is just as important in a collective sense as it is for individual leaders and in group dynamics as well as one-on-one.

With awareness, we can step back and adapt our team working styles; thus, the Sphere of Influence also encourages emotional perceptiveness and self-regulation, key emotional intelligence components of Mayer and Salovey's model. It's a useful tool to have in your kit if you've already got a diverse team but want to further boost your collective intelligence.

WHAT'S NEXT?

In Chapter Two, we discussed how our brains influence our behavior. Here, we've expanded that conversation, discussing how our behaviors influence others. This knowledge is critical because once we better understand how to improve our interactions with others, we can benefit more deeply from the power of Professional Closeness. We can also improve our work environments and boost productivity.

Next, we'll explore more ways to do the same as they relate to combining analytical and design thinking, which I firmly believe is the path forward.

CHAPTER SIX

COMBINING ANALYTICAL AND DESIGN THINKING

Years ago, when BlackBerry roamed the world, a mobile phone operator in low-income African and Latin American markets asked me to facilitate a rollout. It was aiming to kick-start a change in its corporate mindset. Initially, before mobile data was mainstream, the company had a singular technical focus: to create and support a network that would give reliable cellular technology access to people in these areas. There were many data-minded leaders and engineers on the team—all very effective linear, analytical thinkers. As the company grew and the world changed, the "customer" side of things began to become more important. Customers no longer just wanted network coverage; that was a hygiene factor. Now they wanted features.

My team was invited to help these strong analytical leaders become more consumer-centric. We traveled to Bolivia to get started, right before Carnival. Ultimately, we decided against approaching the facilitation in the traditional way; this time, there would be no PowerPoints, no spreadsheets. Yes, they understood that language. They understood numbers. The point of our whole intervention, though, was to open their eyes to what they *didn't* understand. So we tailored our messages in a way that would shake things up.

We gathered the executives into teams and had them talk to real-life customers on the streets. They asked basic questions: What was their user experience like? What features would they like to see?

While the questions themselves weren't groundbreaking, the physical act of asking them seemed to be a huge eye-opener. Mingling with consumers who actually used their products was something none of them had done before. Suddenly, answers to analytical questions like, "Is your connection reliable?" became stories about adult children keeping in touch with aging parents and mothers feeling confident they could get medical care for their children in emergencies.

While this first exercise brought emotion into the mix and challenged executives to sideline their analytical tendencies, the second exercise brought that linear thinking back in. We gave the leaders two hours and asked them to dissect the organization's internal issues, breaking problems down incrementally. We had them identifying specific elements that were and were not working, taking notes, and mapping potential causations.

Then we brought the exercise full circle and asked them to re-engage their creative and emotional sides. We instructed everyone to invite three or four colleagues from across the company to come to a theater show— El Teatro—in two and a half hours. The catch was that the show hadn't yet been designed, and the headlining actors were the executives themselves. The same ones who, hours before, had been in the streets talking to customers, then analyzing and charting. Their mission? To combine the insights they had gathered outside—about customer expectations and use cases—with what they learned inside from dissecting company-wide problems. Then, of course, they had to portray it in a way fitting to theater.

Many of them panicked. It was one of the most fun experiences I've ever had as a facilitator—and I can say that now, because it worked. It worked so well that we've repeated the process seven times.

Although some were reluctant to get up on stage, they did.

They put skin in the game. They brought Carnival-style singing, storytelling, and dancing to the task that had challenged them before: putting themselves in the shoes of the customer. After the session, there was a palatable shift in energy; hearts, eyes, and minds were opened. **Now, they were willing to put initiatives in place for a strategy that not only helped their customers but helped their company stay relevant.** The ripple effects were long-lasting.

TWO SCHOOLS OF THOUGHT, MERGED INTO TACTICS

Design thinking—which I also like to call intuitive thinking—in an organization is the opposite of how business is usually conducted. For example, the old way of doing things looks like this: someone has an idea or plan, and the group is convinced it will be fantastic. The organization tests, prototypes, and markets the shiny new idea in the spirit of proving itself right, shepherding the idea through even if it might not be the best way forward. Or even solve the right problem in the first place.

Why? It all comes back to how our brains function. If you're convinced something will work, and you've taken steps to convince your team, too, you are closely connected to the core of that idea. Instead of looking at the idea holistically or critically to improve upon it, you develop loss aversion. You push it through, even if it's not the best. Another problem here is that the more energy, resources, money, and time you pour into a single idea early on, the bigger the risk of failure. This is how businesses and organizations become stagnant—or worse.

When an organization approaches problem-solving or ideation with a design thinking mindset, on the other hand, the most successful idea—the idea that wins—is often a Frankenstein's monster of many earlier ideas. In other words, a hybrid of many previous ideas that have been critically tested, challenged, and adapted. In these scenarios, you aren't working to prove yourselves right; you're working to find the best solution that solves the right problem. The problem you've identified by analyzing your customers' needs and pains.

This is not to say analytical or traditional thinking does not have a place in business; quite the opposite, actually. Analytical thinking states you must have data and facts, both of which help you create situational awareness. Analytical thinkers believe if you have a strong sense of your surroundings, you then have an idea of the terrain and how it relates to the bigger context. **Put simply, analytical thinking states, "if you can't measure it, then it doesn't exist." Design thinking calls bullshit, saying, "it's not that it doesn't exist—it just doesn't exist *yet*."**

Neither is wrong.

Both analytical and design thinking are valid approaches to business, and both are only part of the puzzle when applied on their own. Combining the two, then, is not only the right decision but the table stakes to remaining relevant. Think, for example, of your business strategy as a journey you take by foot. You start walking from where you are, obviously, so you need situational awareness of exactly where that is and what that looks like. **As you begin to walk, though, you will have to start thinking about when you'll make your next turn and what could be around the bend, tapping into more creative and intuitive sources.** Once you make a directional shift, you'll recall that situational awareness back into play—and so forth. **Good business practice is to know where you are but also to take the time to constantly look ahead; combining these skillsets is the path forward.** Alternatively, we can look at the issue from an organizational perspective. To respond more strategically to the changing demands of the business environment, we need to use design thinking, too—which often gets left by the wayside. Merging the two helps us move beyond analytical reasoning when we craft future directions and acknowledge that objective assessments of the past won't necessarily reflect future business realities.

Similarly, competitive advantage means trying to create synergistic value. Logically, that can only happen when strategic approaches view the firm as more than "the sum of its parts"—when we combine intuitive, holistic thinking with rational and analytical approaches.

When it comes to strategy, then, holistic and analytical thinking both play a role in boosting adaptability, helping us design "bigger picture" strategies for the future.

Note that as a leader, you need not house both schools of thought in your brain equally, although it couldn't hurt. Instead you must be self-aware and socially perceptive enough to recognize each skillset in others and create teams that can leverage the benefits of both, creating an environment ripe for high degrees of collective intelligence. The magic is in the balance. Let's explore two schools of thought that illustrate just that.

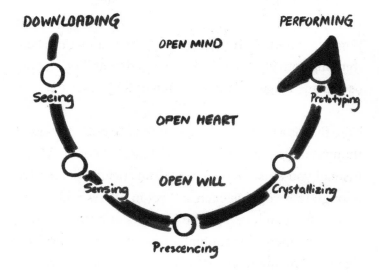

For his book *Theory U*, Otto Scharmer surveyed 45,000 people across the world for over seven weeks in order to understand, in his words, "the self and nature, the self and others, and the self and self." Relevant to our discussion of design thinking and driving organizations forward, Scharmer discovered that **many leaders don't dare to ask themselves one critical question: What is the future I want to be a part of? Instead, individuals and teams get locked into a pattern of "downloading from the past," or habitual repetition.** Those who subscribe to this way of thinking, consciously or subconsciously, believe that if they repeat the same actions over and over, they'll eventually end up with a different result

(Einstein's definition of madness). As we discussed in Chapter Four, this strategy is akin to driving by looking only at your rearview mirror and never your windshield. You won't last long that way.

That said, I understand why many leaders find themselves in this situation. Downloading from the past is a comfortable way to proceed. It is known. A better approach is becoming comfortable with being uncomfortable. This plants the true seeds of growth, and in turn these let you achieve the satisfaction that accompanies Professional Closeness. All the while, of course, helping you move the needle for your business.

You can start shifting your gaze from the rearview mirror to the windshield by first paying attention to others in the vehicle—or the room—with you. Selflessly observe other stakeholders, and do so from their perspective. Removing your judgment widens your peripheral vision, and you'll be better able to reflect on the path forward. You'll be free to think about whether the questions you're trying to answer are even the right questions in the first place. You may find smaller questions beginning to pop up—like seeds, they might grow into a future you want to be part of.

Scharmer's concept is more than theoretical. It points out that you can't simply change your thinking and shift the way things are done—you must act. You must learn by doing. Experiment with new seeds and new fields. With each idea, focus not on spending too much or making everything perfect but rather on execution. Build prototype after prototype. Expect to fail—and fail often—until you arrive at a different future, a different outcome.

In the grand scheme of things, Scharmer applies his Theory U to large issues such as social division and pollution. But here's what's interesting: the same mindsets you need to tackle those mammoth societal hurdles are the ones you need to apply to your organization if you want to move toward a revised, better future. You need the courage to say that a change is needed, and you need to counter greed, fear, and ignorance with love, listening, and trust.

This is easier said than done, but it can be accomplished by shifting, as Scharmer says, "from ego to eco." In other words, instead of hanging on to your ego—instead of staying where it is safe and comfortable—shift your mindset to focus more on the *eco*system around you. When you pay closer attention to context, you can raise your consciousness and stop repeating patterns. Then you can start looking through your windshield and move forward instead of spinning your wheels as a person and as an organization.

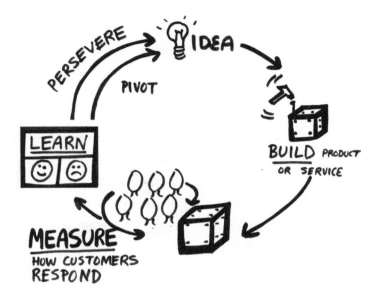

In *The Lean Startup*, Eric Ries shares what has become a wildly popular concept for starting a business—one rooted in a form of strategic caution and baked-in iteration. In a sense, lean development, like Theory U, is about incremental but continuous development, iteration, prototyping, and learning in repeated cycles. Rather than channeling everything into one radical, transformational change, lean firms confront smaller, and much more frequent failures than larger organizations.

Ries believes that rather than try to mirror the way big businesses operate, young companies should start with a minimal viable product first. The "bare bones" in this case come well before companies go full speed ahead, and after the first ideas are built, it's the first place they stop and look around for directions.

Then they should test its success within a select group of customers—focusing not on their intentions but measuring their actual behaviors. Dropbox, for example, released a video of its MVP and used waiting list signups to gauge traction. It gave the then-startup enough time to pivot based on summary statistics—a semi-scientific approach to iterative new product development and learning while doing.

Companies following the lean startup model will repeat the process, modifying the product and testing repeatedly until they have enough tangible information that points to a product success rather than a flop. They build, measure, and learn as fast as possible, rinsing and repeating the cycle as often as it takes. That's not to say they never go to market; in fact they do, numerous times. What they manage, which larger firms may not, is to approach development sustainably. They learn not from the past but from the present, and they don't stop learning or growing. Lean firms use core metrics to validate hypotheses instead, iterating and refining to create real user value.

In other words, Reis advocates increasing the number

of small failures such that it decreases your risk of a big failure. **Because failure is the fuel of growth,** I agree with Ries's premise.

COMBINING TECHNIQUES TO DRIVE RESULTS

In my work facilitating and coaching, I often help clients combine analytical and design thinking, or cognitive and intuitive thinking, using a series of complementary techniques. You can research each of these individually, but the following high-level overviews showcase the interconnectivity of these two schools of thought in action. The specific combination of techniques I'm about to share, I should say, are among my all-time favorites. Note that this is far from an exhaustive list, but it should provide fodder for discussion.

Again, note that in these pairs, the point is not that one method is superior to the other. Rather, the point is to leverage them collectively, creating a level of trust so the whole team can stretch themselves an optimal amount.

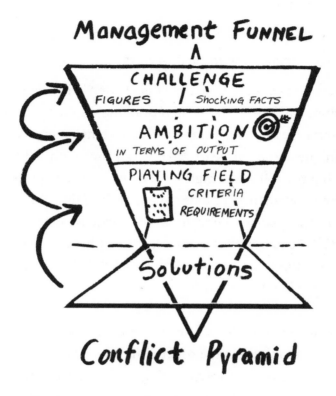

I call this combination of techniques the Swiss Army knife
of management tools because it's a true multi-tool. It's
useful in problem-solving, delegation, conflict resolution,
strategizing, and anytime you simply need to remove
egos from the situation and get on the same page.

The *Management Funnel* technique created by Filip Vandendriessche, as described in his book *Leading without Commanding*, is an analytical tool well-suited for solving a wide range of organizational issues. To start, recall the shape of a funnel. For this exercise, the top of the funnel is the challenge itself, and the bottom is the output. To move through the funnel, first list all the indisputable facts related to the challenge, being as illustrative and honest as possible. Then write an output-oriented statement that speaks to your specific ambition in solving said challenge. Then make an inventory of all criteria that define the playing field; this is the space in which you might look for a solution to reach that output. In other words, these are boundaries you will use to help define your ultimate solution.

For example, your boundaries could be legal or policy requirements that apply to the challenge at hand. It often helps to think of solutions that are unacceptable when defining the playing field, as this is the most direct way to discover the boundaries past which suggestions cannot go. With all these parameters set, any team member can suggest any solution that fits within the designated playing field and does not exceed its limits. It gives a sense of engagement and ownership to those who suggest ideas and brings some objectivity into selecting a solution that otherwise may never have come up.

The *Conflict Pyramid* technique is a conflict resolution

tool that leverages intuitive thinking and has a similar first step: invert the layers of the Management Funnel and apply them to the shape of a pyramid. This time, begin your process at the solution stage. Each time someone presents a solution, work backward. Ask, does the solution fit the playing field? Does the solution solve for the ambition? Each time you hit a "no," stop and question why it doesn't. Discuss the elements of that level and clarify and understand each other's perspectives.

For example, you may have someone from a big organization and someone from a small organization who have come together to make a decision. Both have good ideas—ideas that have worked for them in the past and to which their respective egos are attached. Sticking to these ideas is a breeding ground for conflict, regardless of whether they are good solutions to the problem. In fact, more than 70 percent of client conflicts I've experienced stem from some variant of this dynamic—a negative dynamic this duo of techniques can help break.

For the first technique, the Management Funnel, you would have started with a holistic view of the problem, limited only by a few objective facts. Using the second approach, the Conflict Pyramid, you started with a narrower set of potential "hypotheses" and worked in the opposite direction. Did you end up with the same solutions?

FORCE-FIELD ANALYSIS AND RANDOM OBJECT STIMULI: MAY THE FORCE BE WITH YOU

A second favorite approach of mine is to combine Force Field Analysis with a Random Object Stimuli exercise. *Force Field Analysis* leverages your analytical skills. While originally invented in the field of organizational psychology by Kurt Lewin, its application goes much further.

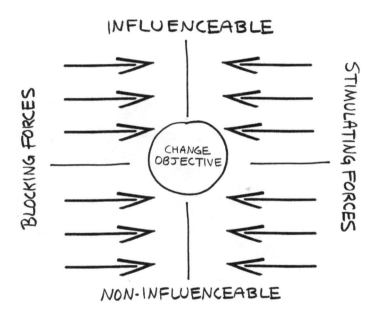

To start, focus on what you want to change about a product or a situation, and make an inventory of forces—people, behaviors, mindsets, and so forth—that are either inhibiting or enabling the change you want to realize. Then rate those forces in order of strength, and examine whether or not you're able to influence or move them in any way. When you're done, you'll have a map that clearly shows what it's most conducive to focus your energy on if you want to arrive at your desired outcome. You'll be able to see, for example, that removing the blockage of a particular force will allow action to flow in the direction you intended. Often, removing or diminishing blocking factors will be all that's needed to get things moving in the right direction.

The *Random Object Stimuli* exercise is a tool aimed at sparking creativity. The exercise leverages intuitive thinking and can help you find solutions to rid yourself of the blockage you identified with force field analysis. To start, choose a random object—a stapler, a book, anything near you. Ideally, put the object in the middle of a large blank canvas, or you can even place it in the center of a room and hand out Post-It notes to participants. Everyone then writes down characteristics associated with that object, both actual characteristics and what it isn't. The point of the exercise is to use combinations of seemingly random words to spark ideas and solutions you never would have found otherwise. If no solutions either fit the parameters or seem helpful, use new combinations of words. When finding new and creative solutions, the biggest challenge is to create enough ideas in the first place to get past the layer of predictability.

Most strategizing techniques start with identifying deficits then coming up with ways to address those gaps— needs analysis, TOWS strategizing, SWOT—the list goes on. We're more familiar in general with these, and, as I've suggested, analysis comes more naturally to most of us. By complementing it with holistic thinking in the Random Object Stimuli exercise, we're opening up possibilities again. How did you feel about each?

ACTIVITY-BASED COSTING AND VALUE PROPOSITION CANVAS: THE WHAT MEETS THE WHY

Activity-Based Costing is an analytical technique that helps companies that are struggling to increase profit margins or facing a similar financial challenge. To start, take an organizational activity and list all the elements in the chain of sales related to that organizational activity. For example, if you run an airline, ask yourself how customers receive their boarding passes. Then list the organizational costs of each incremental action. This gives you a rational overview of how funds are allocated.

The *Value Proposition Canvas* created by Alexander Osterwalder is a technique on the intuitive side that speaks to the *why* first, not the what. To start, identify your ideal customer segment and consider what their jobs-to-be-done are outside of, but related to, your service.

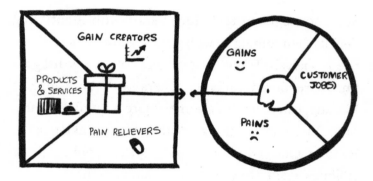

For example, if you run an airline company, you can assume customers do more than simply walk on board your plane. Incrementally, they also book a flight, pay for the flight, download a book to read on the flight, pack their laptops, and so much more. Ask yourself what pains and gains exist in the customer experience outside of your core value proposition and how you can help make the customer happy in an unexpected way. When you have your list, compare it to the one you created during

Activity-Based Costing. What blockages do you see? What opportunities are there to improve the margin or add value? The goal here is to optimize the customer's experience while simultaneously taking the company's cost structure into account. Leveraging both will generate more than just financial profits for your organization.

This one was not too far removed from the mobile phone executives' experience. Activity-Based Costing invited you to see your organization as separate parts, segments, or operations. Putting yourself in a consumer's shoes for the second exercise was an invitation to view your company as a symbiotic creator of value. Do you feel that it built on the first? How?

WHAT'S NEXT?

You don't have to give an interpretive dance at Carnival to improve how you communicate and function as an organization. (Although, I admit, it would be fun.) When used together, analytical and design thinking—and the various strategies that fall under their respective umbrellas—can encourage more Professional Closeness within teams. As I've also seen time and again in my work with clients, it creates a deep and holistic understanding of the business context.

In the next chapter, I'll first ask you to take a hard look at your effectiveness as a leader and your overall progress as an organization. Then we'll examine specific strategies you can use to improve both.

You may want to get your pen. I'll wait.

CHAPTER SEVEN

FIVE STRATEGIES FOR POSITIVE CHANGE

It's time to look in the mirror.

Now, you see the value of raising your collective intelligence, breaking down silos, and combining both analytical and design thinking components in your organizational approach. Have you taken steps in that direction? Have you had those tough conversations?

Then look at how you collaborate as an executive team. Are you paying attention to how you show up in interactions? Are you leading effectively? Consider your management of others, too. Do you trust the individual greatness of your team members and give them the space they need to succeed? Or are you micromanaging?

Have you created an environment that's divided, or are your people and functions linked with strong connections?

If you've made it this far, I commend you for wanting to learn more about how to create positive change in your organization. Here are five strategies that can help.

BECOME COMFORTABLE WITH BEING UNCOMFORTABLE

I started here for a reason: many of the concepts I've discussed in this book thus far have likely felt foreign to you. Guess what? The following strategies probably will, too—

and that's okay. In fact, that's a good thing. There is no linear path to using the power of Professional Closeness; the journey is not of the A-to-Z variety. **Some concepts will resonate with you more than others, but regardless of which those are, one fact remains: in order for you to grow, you must become comfortable with being uncomfortable.** This is not easy; it requires you to take your ego out of the equation and show a level of transparency and vulnerability many leaders have unconsciously calloused over. Hardest of all, it requires you to take these difficult actions consciously and in the moment, which can feel even scarier.

How can you do this, exactly? **When you start to get that sinking feeling in your stomach, flip the frame: use that as a signal of encouragement.** Let it show you that you're entering into a conversation, situation, or thought pattern that is new. Lean into the knowledge that these new approaches are what bring new results; they're where the future starts. Do this once. Then do it the next time, too. As with all behaviors, the more you respond differently, the more likely your brain is to learn that reaction as a pattern, not an anomaly. In other words, each time you lean in, it's a building block for your agility as a leader and, subsequently, as an organization.

Remember, though, that not every uncomfortable situation has a positive outcome; just because something is challenging doesn't mean it will simply work by default. Paramount to leveraging the ability to become comfortable with being uncomfortable as a skill is embracing failure, not running from it. **In fact, facing a level of failure that you'd rather avoid is inevitable when you're striving for anything really worth something.** It means that what you're doing really is new to you and you're doing it right.

UNDERSTAND THAT TIME IS THE NEW CURRENCY

Time is the most important finite resource we have as individuals. Rather than focusing on tired terms like "work-life balance" and similar, it's a better approach to examine time as a currency. Let's bring our analytical thinking into play and look at time like we would any other budget item: globally, employees work an average of forty-four weeks out of the year. If we use the typical forty-hour week schedule in our calculation, that means we each work around 1,760 hours per calendar year.

You've likely heard of the 10,000-Hour Rule popularized by Malcolm Gladwell—that is, that in order to reach a level of expertise in something, you need to spend at least 10,000 hours working on it. (Recall that failures are inevitable. I didn't say 10,000 hours of success; just 10,000 hours of work.) Similarly, moving from "novice" to "competent" takes one hundred hours. In a business sense, I believe that in today's marketplace, a team should be operating between the levels of competent and expert to be considered high-performing.

What does this mean to you? Say you work as a manager in a typical company with a classic operating structure; every two weeks, you get together with other managers to discuss operations, short-term actions, and commercial results. If you're lucky, part of this conversation is about company strategy and direction. You spend the rest of your time on your day-to-day tasks. In this all-too-common scenario, that means you are spending only fifty-two hours a year or less on tasks that help you collectively lead the company into the future. According to the 10,000-Hour Rule, that won't even get you to "competent."

This perspective is meant to be empowering, not discouraging. When you look at time as currency, you can be more cognizant of using it effectively rather than simply going through the motions. For example, you could not only rethink the focus, design, and content of your management meetings, but you could also encourage other groups within your organization to come together. Consider strategic and not merely task-based sessions when they do, and think about working to understand the heart or root of problems. Look at them from different angles. Recall Amazon's two-pizza rule? Many small teams working together not only helps you leverage collective intelligence but can also exponentially increase the number of hours your organization as a whole is spending on building expertise and moving forward.

In addition, analyzing time from a budget perspective can help you justify more tangible line items. For example, many remotely working leaders may need to travel to one location for a week-long strategy meeting, which is a substantial expense for your organization—travel, lodging, time away from projects, and so forth. Challenge yourself:

Can you see past those perceived line-item deficits? Can you compare them to the potential positives of having thinkers spending face time together for the benefit of the company's future? Can you assign a perceived value to those figures, just as you would any other item on your spreadsheet? Can you understand the associated travel costs are investments, and not just expenditures? When you start viewing time as a budget item, you're one step closer to a holistic approach.

Looking at time as a currency can also help you create a rhythm of growth in your company. For example, it takes four to six weeks to learn a new behavior—that is, to grow new neuropathways connected to that action or skill. **If you don't allocate your time such that you allow for this deep learning, any change you implement may only be short-lived.** Ultimately, how you allocate your time means far more than how you create a schedule; doing so intentionally helps form the social structure and cognitive dynamic you need to create real change.

Zooming in and out essentially means unlearning something you've likely held on to for some time: the idea that you always have to be on top of everything and know what everyone in your organization is doing. That you have to know exactly what's going on at all times. That you have to have a hand in each initiative, each decision, and each move. I understand why you feel this way; for years, you've been trying to see the big picture—to maintain a bird's-eye view—while remaining caught up in the weeds. Doing both simultaneously is an impossible task, and the sooner you realize it, the better.

Eagles switch focus quickly and easily; they can zoom in on prey opportunities when needed and zoom back out to scan their environments, which keeps them on track. Instead of micromanaging, be more like an eagle than a helicopter. This means zoom in when it counts, and then zoom out to keep an eye on the big picture. How do you know when it counts? That's the crux of being an effective leader. Which details impact your organization the most? What next move(s) are you contemplating, and what information can you zoom in on to make sure it's the right one?

The zoom-in muscle is relatively easy to build because you've likely been flexing it quite often. The zoom-out muscle, though? That's a different story. Even though it may be uncomfortable at first, zoom out wide—not seeing just what your organization is doing as a whole but what your competition is doing, too. What the market is doing. What other markets are doing. Make a conscious effort to work both muscles to increase your overall strength as a leader and as a company.

USE SHOCKING FACTS TO PERSUADE AND LEAD

As a leader, sometimes you need to make a point in a big way. Most often, a boring old spreadsheet or slideshow just won't cut it. Sometimes, you want to inspire your team and get people as excited about an idea as you are; that way, you can open the doors for further innovation and team engagement.

But how? One technique is to use shocking facts to persuade and lead. The concept is straightforward: instead of using many small data points in your delivery, make it have an emotional impact. Make it tangible. Relate it in a way that your team can't help but visualize the impact of your words.

I want to be very clear here: these shocking facts do not mask the challenges or oversell the benefits of your point. There is nothing misleading about presenting rational facts in an emotionally charged way—a way that speaks to the imagination and gets people's attention. You're simply making it more relevant by activating people's emotional mammalian brains. That's leadership, and it's much more effective (and fun) than spouting off numbers to make your case.

Here are three examples of what shocking facts look like:

1. **Saving for sofas.** I worked with a furniture company that was attempting to enter a new market—one with a completely different demographic and drastically decreased economic spending power. After reviewing the data, leaders *could have* reported that they needed to lower prices by a specific percentage to sell the target for the quarter, based on the findings of the market research. Instead, they made it relevant, encouraging their team to dramatically pivot on price (or reconsider the idea altogether) by saying, "It

would take an average customer in the current target market thirty-six months to save up for our lowest-priced sofa."

2. **Build or bust.** Another business-to-consumer company saw its customers' needs were quickly outgrowing its organization's capabilities. So it turned to market research to understand its long-term market potential. Instead of spouting dry statistics about customer engagement quotients and consumer traffic, the company framed it this way: "If we don't dramatically change how we reach our potential customers, it will take us eighteen years to build up the stores to reach them."

3. **Missing out on multiple Mercedes.** I once worked with a pharmaceutical company that manufactured fertility drugs. Gathering the raw material for its product was a time-consuming and expensive process. Managers looked for ways to convince executives to invest in new technology that would speed up development and production. Again, instead of spouting off a spreadsheet, they said, "Each week, we throw away the equivalent in value of three to six high-end Mercedes because we have not invested in new technology installations that would decrease our time to market."

All true, all facts, just presented in a more meaningful way. The ability to appreciate and leverage your knowledge of the human brain is intensely valuable as a leader.

USE SPACE TO CREATE BEHAVIOR

Research from Stanford's School of Design has found that space creates behavior. To understand this concept, let's look at it in action. For a moment, imagine a typical management team convening in a boardroom. What do you see? You may call to mind a long conference table, many chairs, and a projector or whiteboard at the head of the room. Maybe those in the space have their own technology—laptops or tablets—or even simply note-pads and pens. They're all prepared to listen and digest information, and the vibe in the room feels serious. In other words, these meeting participants—before the meeting even starts—are prepared to activate their analytical brains, all based merely on the design of the room. They're prepared to be quiet and listen, automatically falling into a hierarchical pattern that leaves most as passive in the interaction. It's clear to everyone in the room, before a word is even uttered, that whoever is at the head of the table—or whoever is about to stand and present information—is taking the active role.

If you want to leverage collective intelligence, that needs to change. If you want to reap the benefits of operating from a place of Professional Closeness, that needs to change. If you want to forge connections that truly help your organization operate more holistically, that needs to change. I have good news: Stanford's design experts say it *can* change, but not by changing the human makeup of the group—it's by changing the physical space.

Now picture that same group in a different room; the long table is gone, replaced by furniture small enough to be rearranged based on the parameters of the meeting. Instead of one projector or whiteboard at the head of the room flanked by a wall of windows, the room is built for movement. There is space for creativity. For ideation. For people to be both active and passive in interactions—sometimes back and forth in the same conversation—adjusting to other people and the dynamics at play. Their attitudes are determined by the context and objective, not simply the space itself. This type of environment is ripe for design thinking.

You may be skeptical that changing a table and adding some extra whiteboards could improve communication, but it can; I've seen it happen. And I'm not alone. A recent Harvard study ranked 36,000 scientific papers; those papers that scored highest in terms of innovation all were produced in coworking spaces. That is no coincidence; these collaborative spaces were designed to feel more like blank canvases than traditional rooms. These were mainly multipurpose spaces and coworking locations, where professionals could gather all their energy into the same physical space. Where they could work collaboratively and feel higher degrees of ownership over the issues being discussed.

What if, in both rooms we described, meeting-goers were attempting to solve for the same objective? The first boardroom we described felt more like a museum of what is, dipped dangerously into "sage on the stage" territory, and created an environment that didn't inspire confidence or new ideas. The second room we described felt like a hotbed of productivity and allowed leaders to both analyze data and problem solve in a way that felt fresh and opened the door for new ideas. If this were your team, which room would you want it to be in? Which would produce the best outcome?

The bottom line? If you're not getting the behavior you want out of your team, change the space.

WHAT'S NEXT?

If any of these strategies excites you, good. If any made you uncomfortable, even better. Use them to grow as a leader and to empower your team to grow, too, as a unit. That, after all, is the crux of leveraging the power of Professional Closeness to propel your newly holistically functioning organization into a future you can all be proud of.

CONCLUSION

On December 26, 2004, a tsunami hit the Indian Ocean. Substantial parts of the coastal areas were devastated, and there were hundreds of thousands of fatalities. In one tribe of indigenous Sea Gypsies, though, everyone survived.

How?

After the fact, the Sea Gypsies explained that when fishermen of other villages went about their day-to-day lives, they were mainly looking to do one thing: hook fish. It wasn't a negative; after all, they had to eat. And so the surrounding tribes planned their boat routes around hooking fish. They timed their departures to sea around hooking fish. They spent a majority of their focus on hooking fish. They did what they knew.

The Sea Gypsies who all survived the tsunami still sought to feed themselves, but they also focused externally. They reportedly focused on remaining aware of one another as well as the environment around them—in other words, the context—at all times. Before the tsunami struck, they were able to look at the sea and intuitively notice it was changing. They saw how the sea had strangely begun to recede, and that this was followed by an unusually small wave. They saw dolphins flee for deeper water and noticed cicadas fall silent. Because they dived underwater to find food and had adapted to see as well underwater as they had on land, they were keenly aware of changes above and below the surface. They'd immersed themselves in their context. They didn't know *what* was changing—as they had no technology or any type of weather forecast—but they knew it was *something*.

They took their families far out to sea, away from the land the tsunami would eventually ravage. When the devastation was occurring, they were safely on the ocean, miles away.

Why?

Even after the fact, the tribe of fishermen and their families had difficulty putting into words what they saw and why they reacted how they did. To me, it is clear: their situational awareness told them to make a move, and their connection with one another allowed them to shift quickly as a unit.

The tribe had it right: it had closeness, trust, and a big-picture view coupled with the ability to see small patterns that mattered within their context.

Do you?

WHAT'S NEXT?

Your organization may not be facing an impending natural disaster, but you never know what's around the corner. You can get out in front of the damage—and live more happily in the process—by using the tools and concepts I've shared in this book. Remember, though, that Professional Closeness is far more than just a concept; it is a way of operating yourself and your organization that lends itself to real results. However, getting there isn't always intuitive, especially when you consider how we've been conditioned as leaders. I know this because I have spent decades working with clients who have struggled for this very reason, and I've shared many of those examples with you in this book. In the end, though, those who have committed to change have seen real results, both personally and professionally.

How can you do the same? As we discussed in Part I of this

book, the first step is about understanding how you move through the world. How your brain functions, the role your instincts play in your day-to-day life, and how the laws of influence subconsciously affect your impact in interactions. When you more deeply understand yourself, you can begin to break patterns that don't serve you and learn how to use your influence so that it's conducive to growth, not control. Moreover, when you better understand those around you, you can communicate with them in a way that decreases defensiveness and increases collective intelligence.

When you break down communication barriers—often, the most subconscious ones—you can also facilitate the building of connections across silos to reach a level of conscious defragmentation within your organization. This defragmentation is key to taking a holistic approach to your business. It's a decision that, regardless of your industry, can help you not only survive but thrive in this world where we never know what's around the corner. In Part II of this book, I provided many strategies to get you started on that path.

At the end of the day, remember the tribe: as you move forward, hook your fish, connect with your tribe members, and make sure your boats are communicating with one another in a way that allows you to operate as a unit. That way, you're more apt to not only survive but eat well for a lifetime.

ACKNOWLEDGMENTS

This book captures my thoughts and experiences about what I have started calling *Professional Closeness*. It's an action theory in progress, based on my personal journey, and one which I could never have written without the trust of so many clients across the globe. Thanks a million.

I am thrilled to be able to acknowledge those who have helped me become the professional I am today. As I bring this book to a close, these pages are also a very welcome chance to express my heartfelt gratitude to those who helped me along the way and supported me greatly.

The order of these acknowledgments reflects the order in which each person has appeared in my life:

Thanks, Geert Mensing, for hiring me twenty-three years

ago as a junior psychologist. You taught me to always use my own senses, observations, feelings, and impressions rather than place all my emphasis on psychometric questionnaires and other tools. The essence of this basic lesson still guides me today.

Albert Froom, you were an inspiration to me as the leader of a small, high-end consulting firm. You built my professional confidence by giving me the autonomy and responsibility to search principals for a renowned client. The lesson that has stuck with me most, though, is to make sure your existing customers always come first.

Theo van der Tak, I'll never forget how you took me under your wing when I started at Twynstra Gudde. You gave me the responsibility to manage and revive the assessment center practice and always stood behind me. Even though the consultants in that practice area were much older and more senior than I, you helped me find my way and create success on my own terms. I'll never forget your saying: "Laat die gebraden kippetjes maar in je mond vliegen."

Marc Vanschoenwinkel, I've always seen you as a professional mentor and friend. I'm grateful for your loyalty, creative input, and steadiness. You've never let me down and are always there to help. Thanks for showing me how to be a true Organizational Practitioner through the way you coach, do assessments, and train. It remains a pleasure and honor to work with you and to make a difference for our clients.

Dick Webbink, I clearly remember one of the first times we met at Twynstra Gudde, where you were leading the executive search practice. From that first moment, we clicked and have always stayed in contact. Over the years, you have shown your trust in me time and again by introducing me to your most valued customers. I now know, more than ever before, how generous you have been by doing so. Petje af!

Carel Maasland, I cannot easily express what you have meant for me and my professional development. In almost all your roles as a human resource executive, you sought me out and engaged me to support you with leadership development and organizational change missions. Your ideas and energy have always brought out the best in me. Together we have made real impact and created sustainable change. I would like to thank you from the bottom of my heart for all the adventures we have shared. Although I'm not so sure about that time when we crossed the Mara Salvatruca and crime-infested Guatemala-El Salvador border by car ;-).

Marlies Zeeuwen, we first met when I was allowed to join you as co-trainer for the *Lessons In Leadership* program. That program, your wisdom, and the way you apply therapeutic and deep psychological knowledge in leadership development has been a huge inspiration and example for how I approach my assignments today. What stands out is to always see the individual in the context of the group or the team. I deeply respect that you are still going strong in the field of organizational development with forty-five years of experience under your belt.

Michel Koppen, the first time we met, I interviewed you as a store manager, unaware that we'd later be working together on many memorable occasions. You continually pushed me to be pragmatic and never let me get away with advice, programs, or any other work that wasn't 100 percent business-driven. At the same time, your reliance on my expertise continues to be a great privilege.

Of course, I can't close without thanking you, my love, Nik. You are always supporting me, challenging me, and encouraging me to act on my ideas. Since the very start, I have felt you with me every step of the way. As a coach, developer, and test publisher, you inspire me with your tenacity, creativity, and drive. To be absolutely clear— if you hadn't insisted on my taking the leap to actually write the book, it would never have happened. Dank je wel liefste.

Madelon Schrama, you can't imagine how good it feels to know that you're guarding the castle when I'm traveling so much. Your loyal, practical, and hands-on help creates the peace of mind I need to bring my A-game wherever I go. Thank you, Madelon.

These acknowledgments would not be complete without thanking you, Erik Dirven. First of all, I really appreciate your inviting me to help facilitate all those big cultural transformation journeys. The experience and learnings have been invaluable. The thing that stands out most and both inspired and triggered me to expand my thinking is to always pull in the context and think big.

Almost last, but definitely not least, I want to thank you, Marino Maganto. Thank you for trusting me and allowing me and my team to help build a high-performing executive team and a high-performing organization. Working with you and your team has shaped and honed the way I think about Professional Closeness. It's an honor to work with a true leader such as you. Having said that, I also want to thank all the team members who have let us guide and facilitate. Thanks Farid, Elisa, Isabel, Adil, Nawal, Andrea, Sergio, Wojciech, Carsten, Rachida, Ahmad, Adil, Kirsty, Judith, Emile, and Mister Paul.

I want to thank the Scribe publishing team for creating a process that allowed me to express my thoughts and transform them into my first book. The process has been more insightful than I could ever have anticipated.

I feel blessed and happy because I feel as though I have received double the value I expected: a completed book I can feel proud of and an unforgettable experience along the way. Thanks, Jessica, for allowing me to have my own tempo and rhythm. Most of all, I will miss spitballing with you.

Finally, I want to thank you, Cath, for being the best help I could wish for in reviewing the manuscript and helping me reach the finish.

ABOUT THE AUTHOR

GOVERT VAN SANDWIJK is the founder and managing partner of Time to Grow Global, a boutique consultancy that assists organizations with strategy development, HR management, leadership development, and personal growth. Time to Grow Global is truly global, delivering value in over forty countries. Govert leverages his decades of experience and background in organizational psychology to help teams see what is going on beneath the surface, resolve challenges, and ultimately grow. Govert is a consultant, change-maker, facilitator, coach, and entrepreneur. In *The Power of Professional Closeness*, his first book, he shares some of the strategies that have made his approach so successful.

Find out more at http://www.timetogrowglobal.com.